THIS SCRUM MASTER'S NOTEBOOK JOURNAL BELONGS TO:

OBJECTIVE

PROJECT

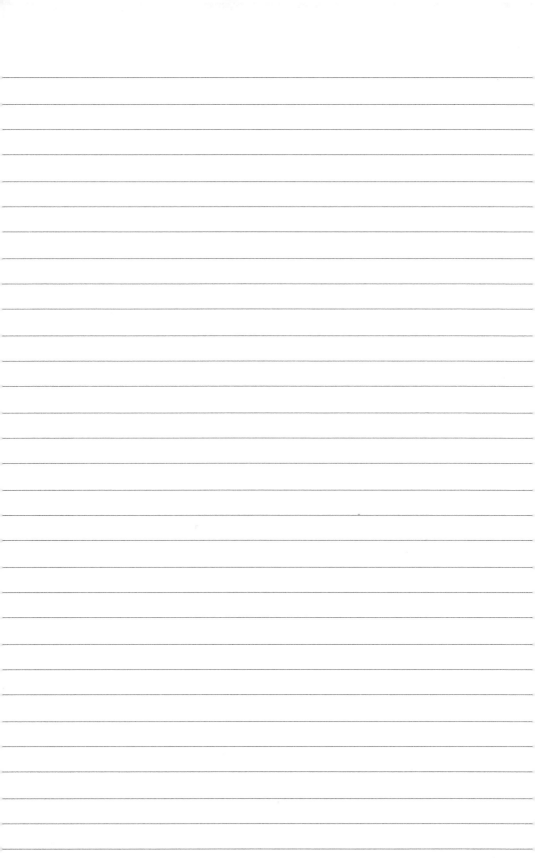

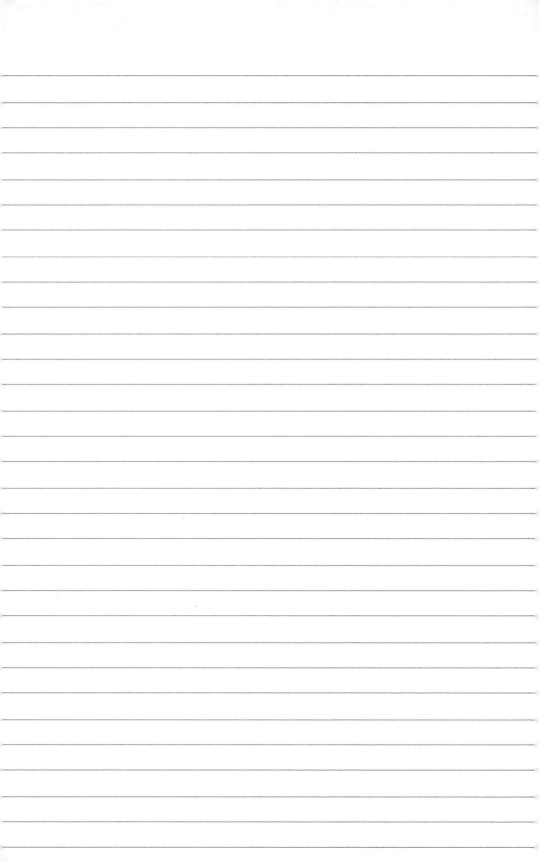

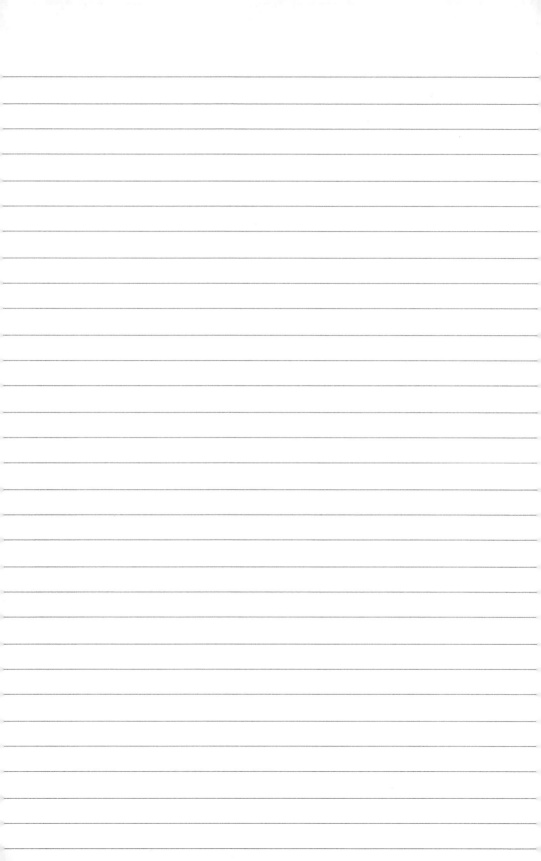

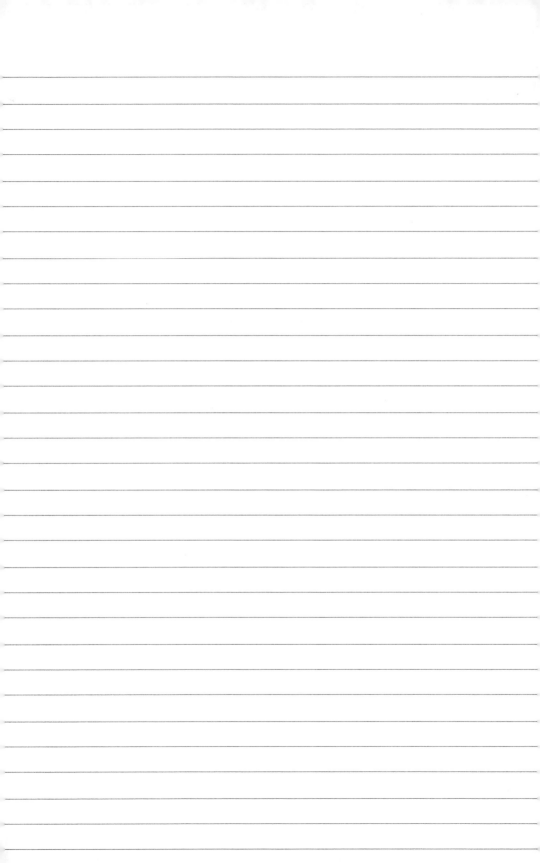

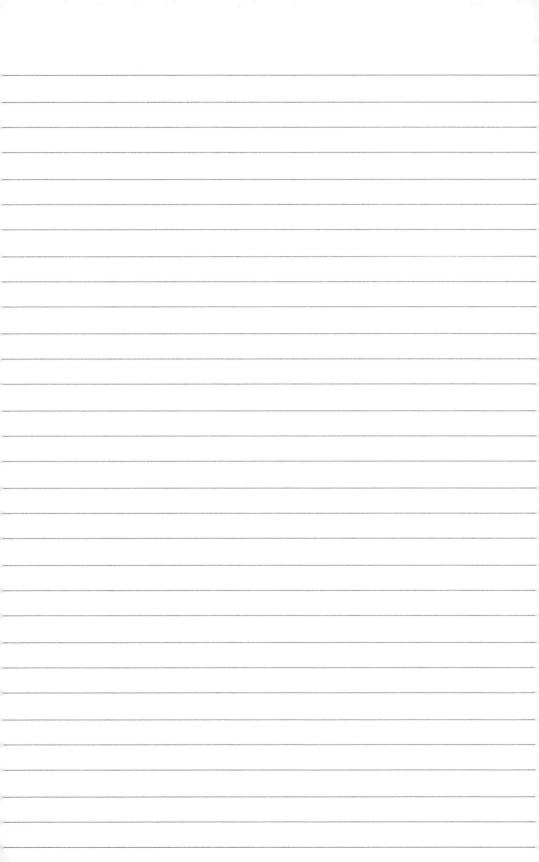

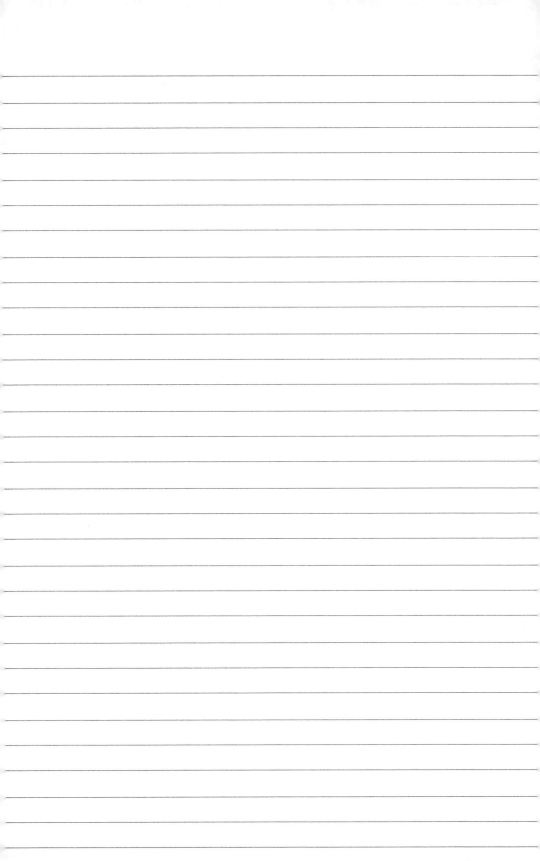

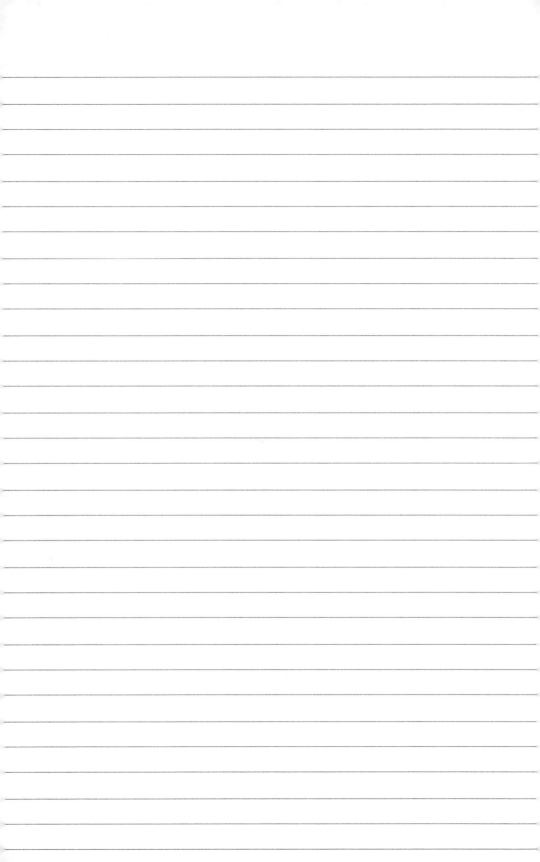

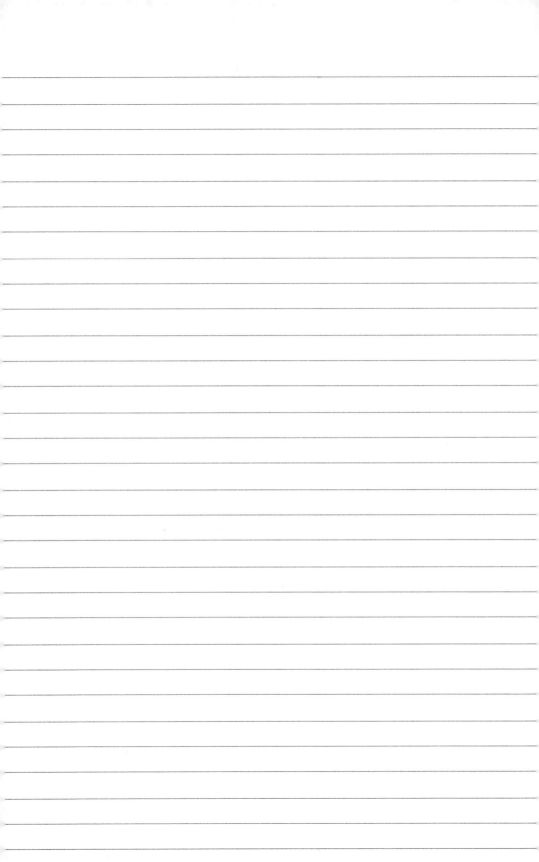

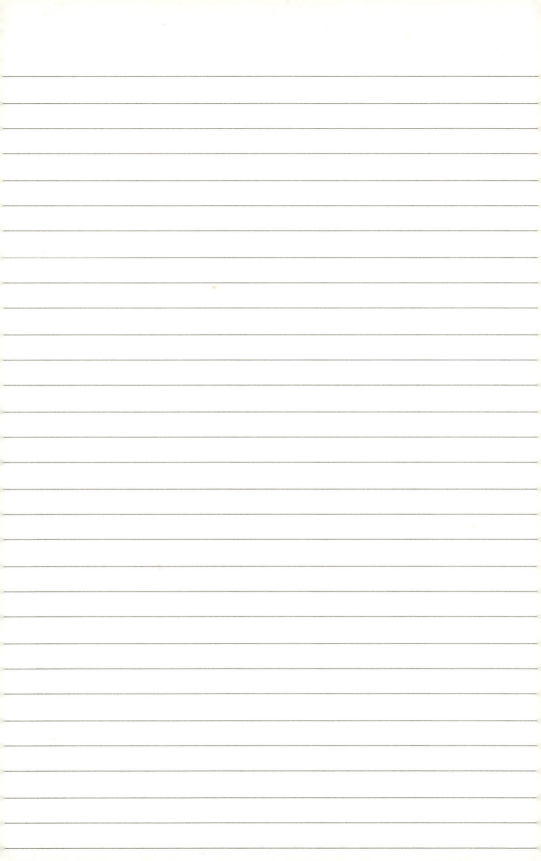

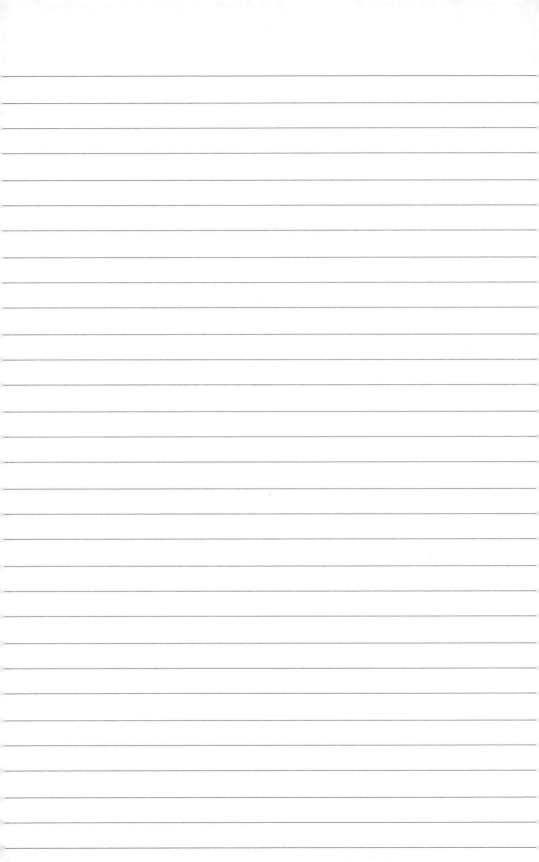

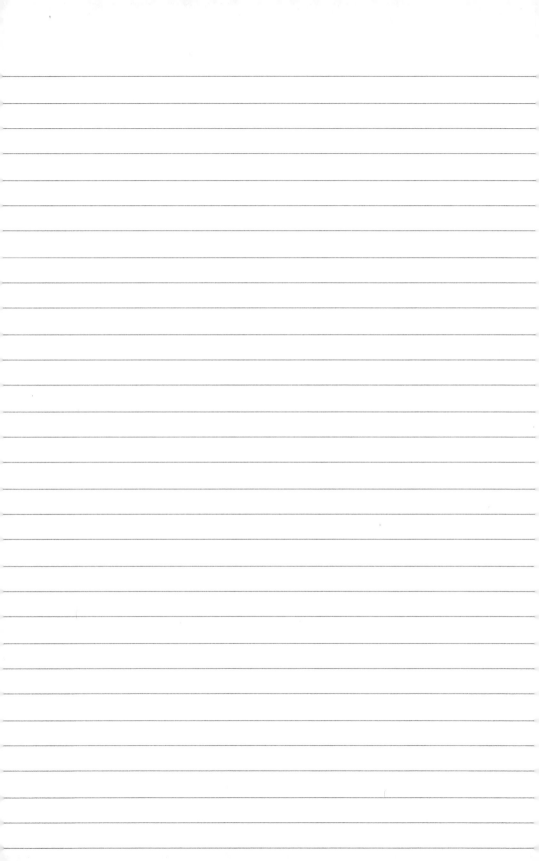

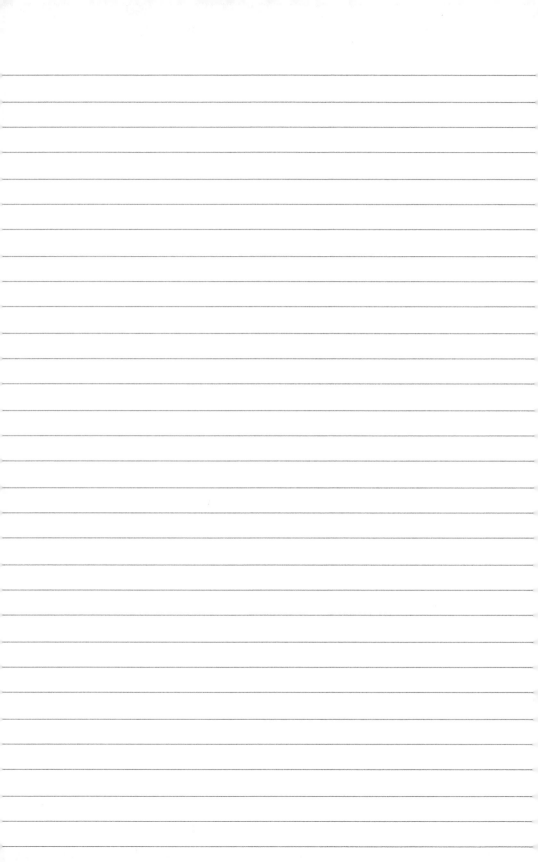

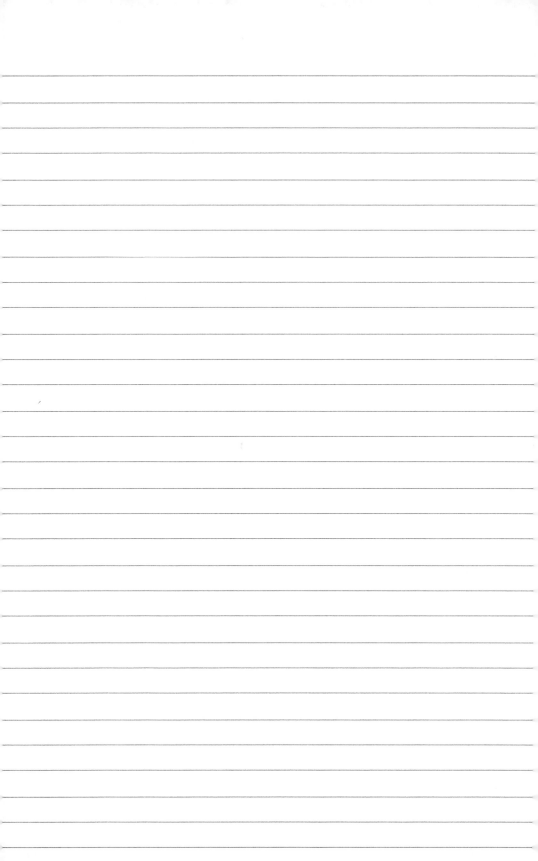

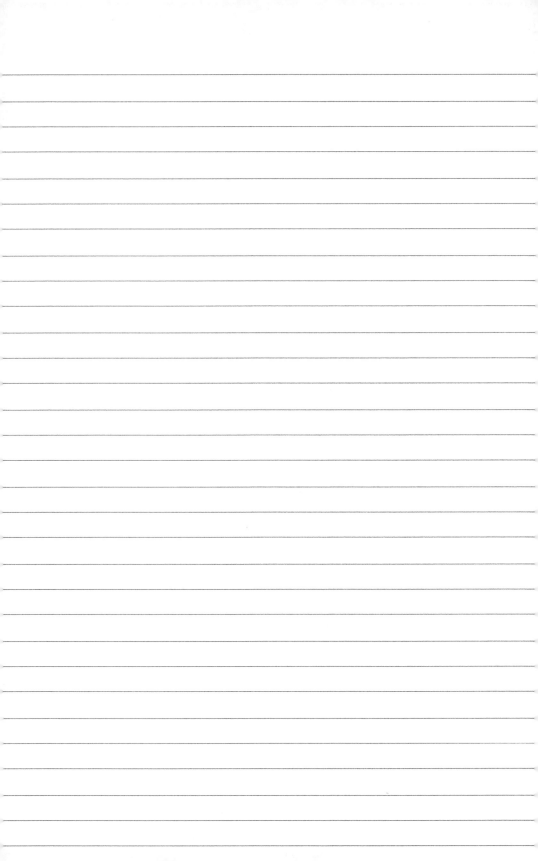

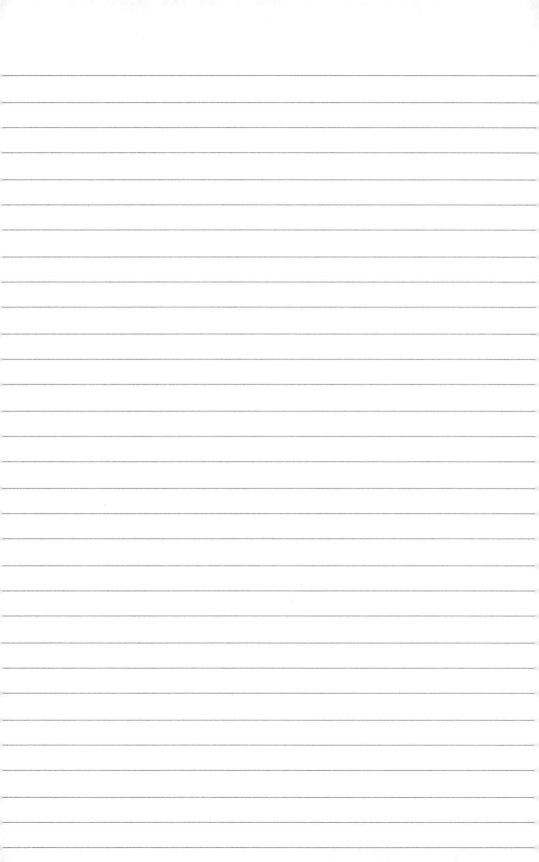

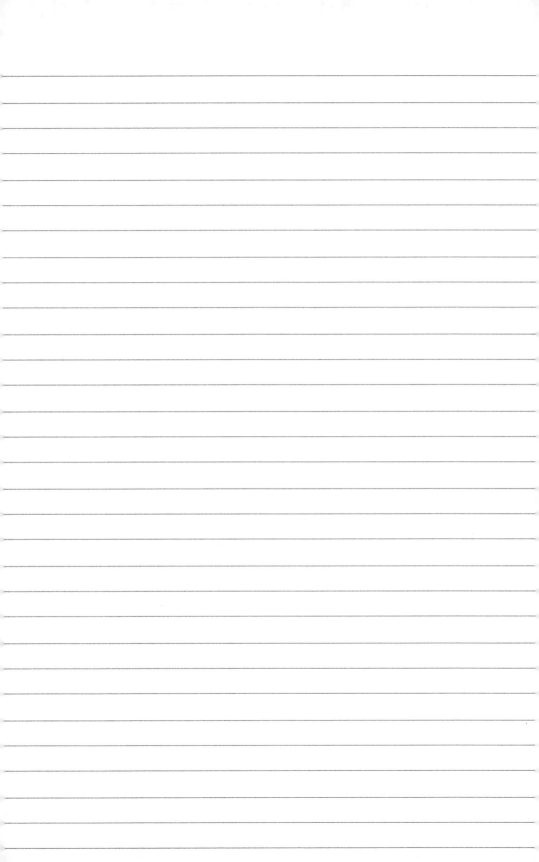

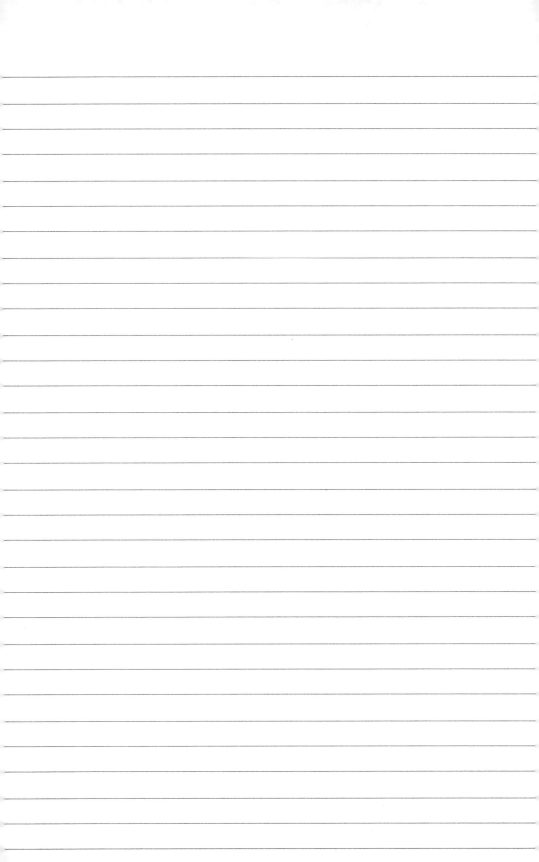

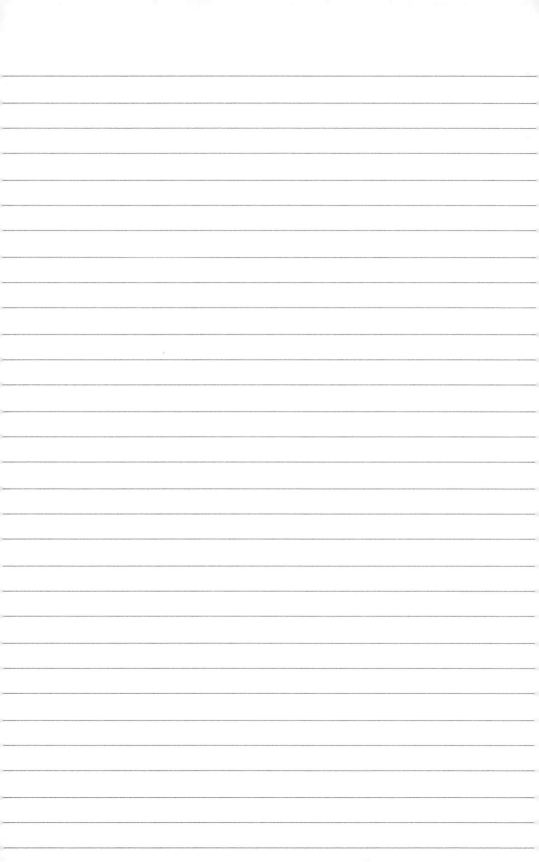

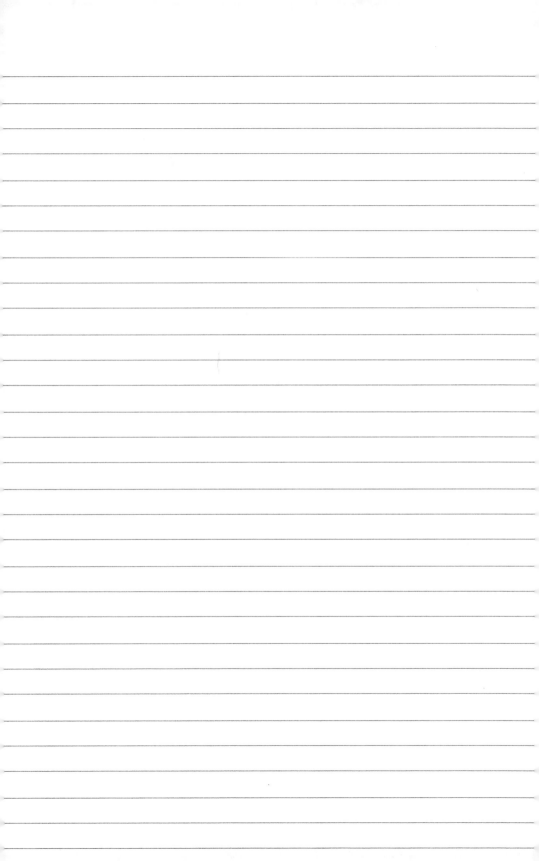

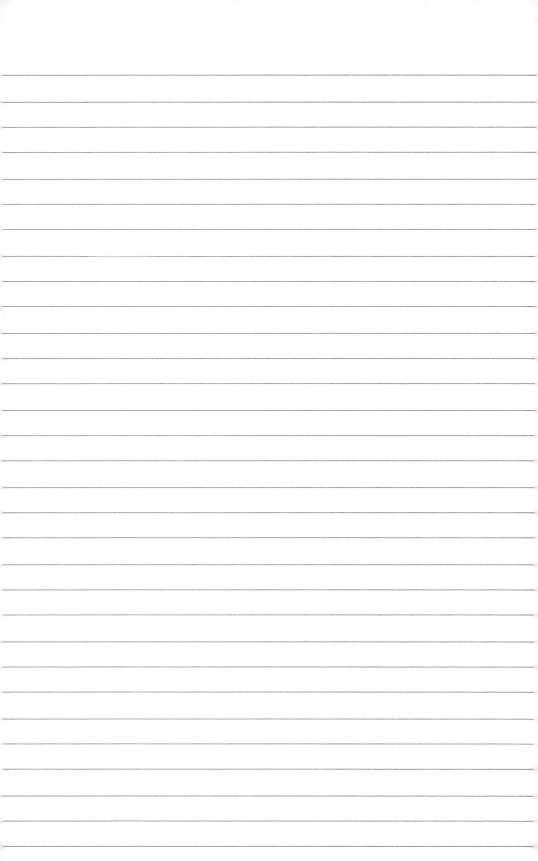

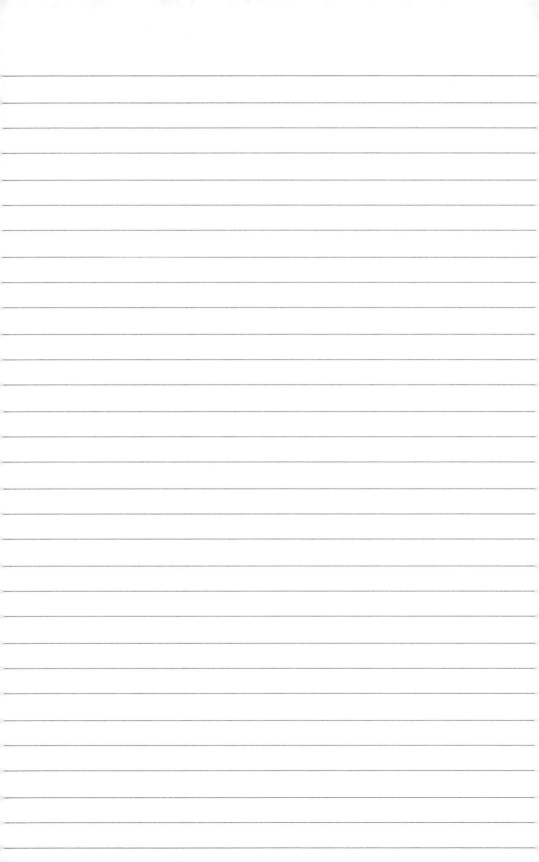

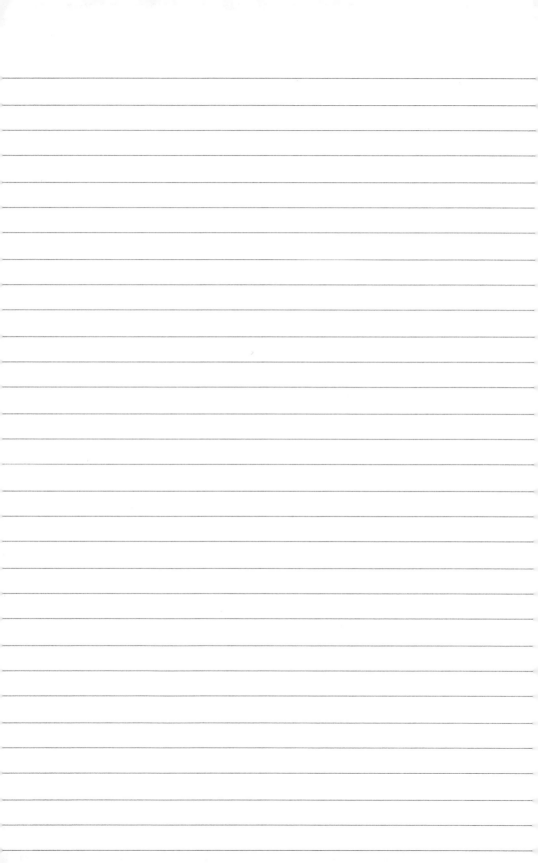

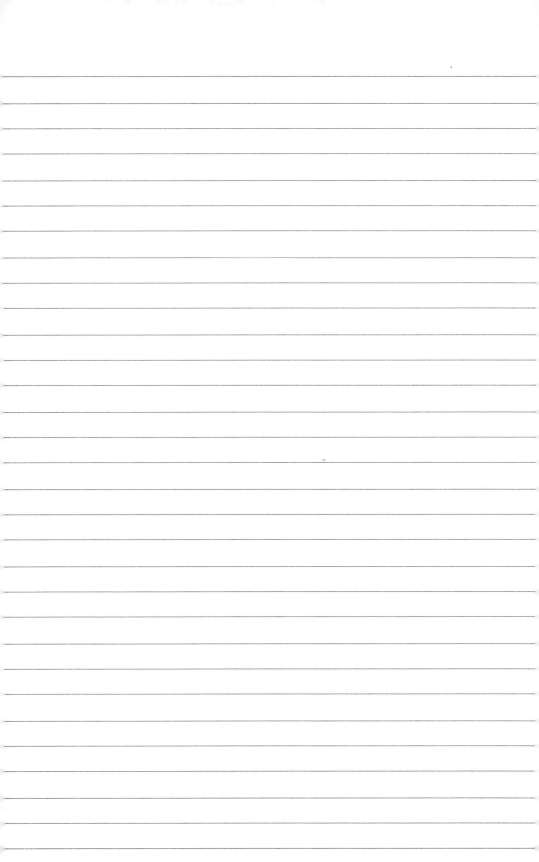

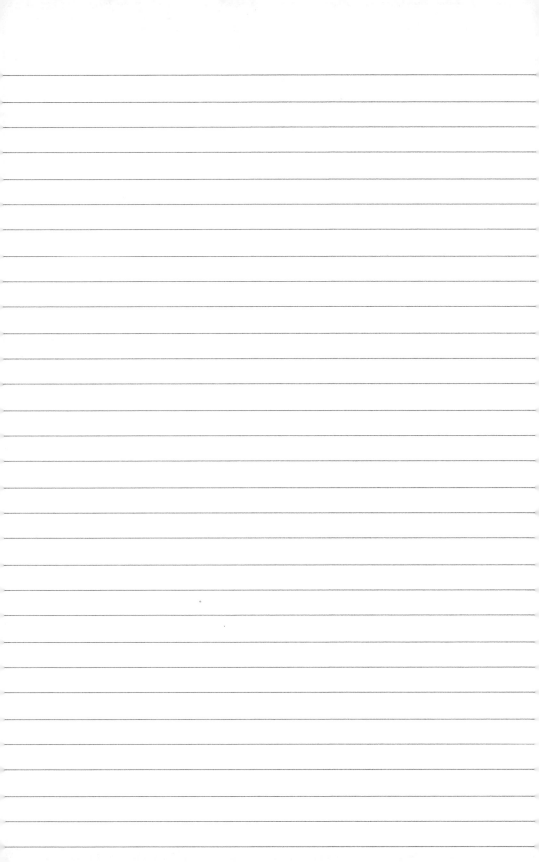

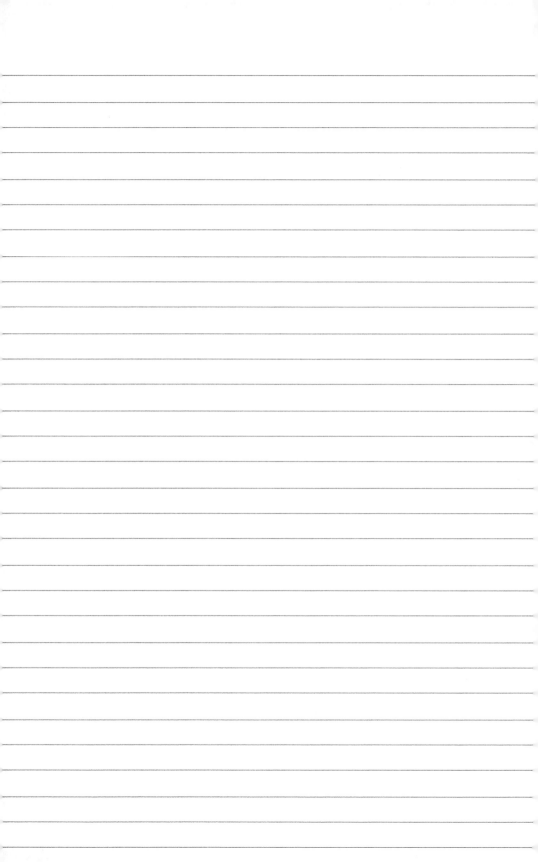

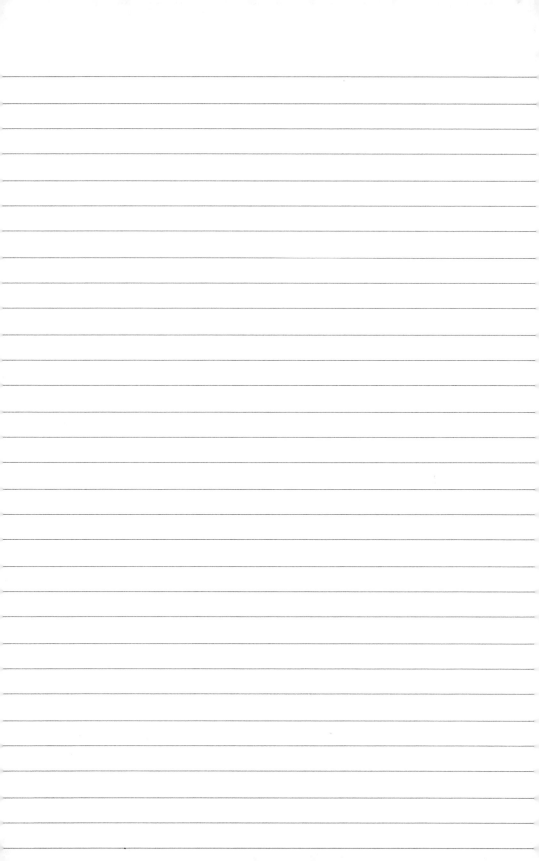

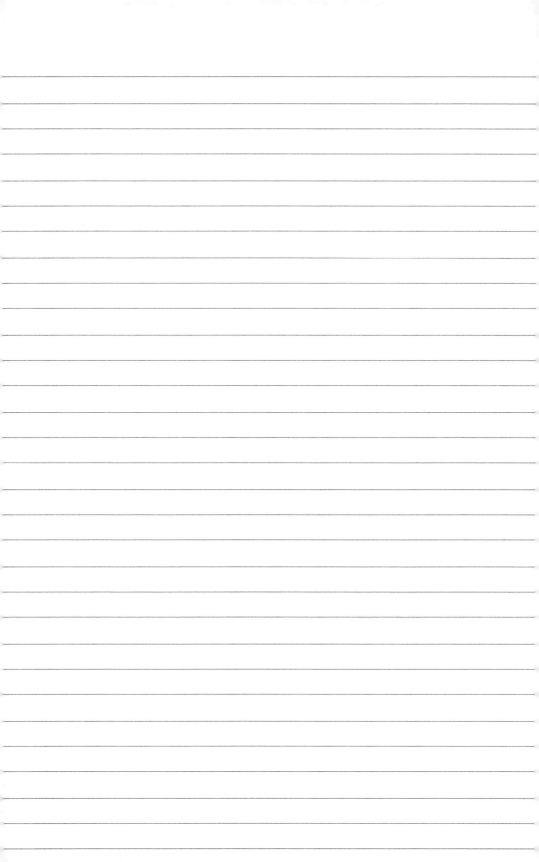

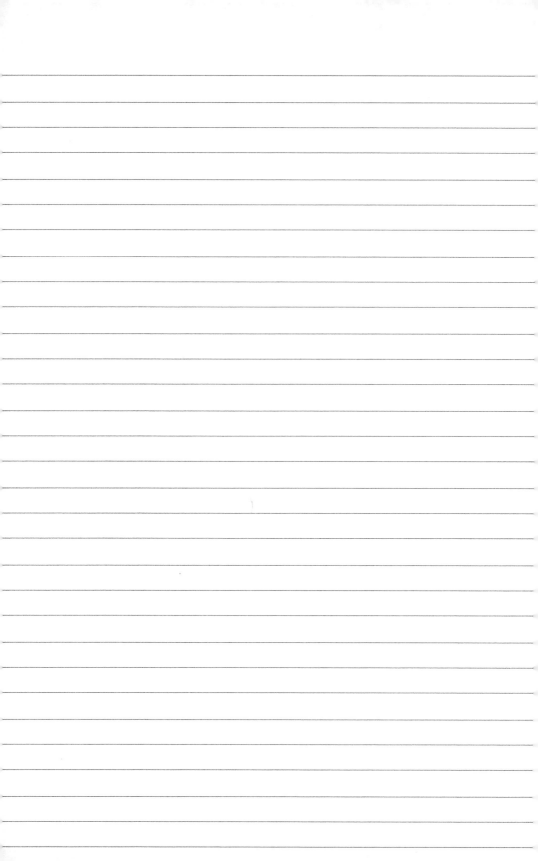

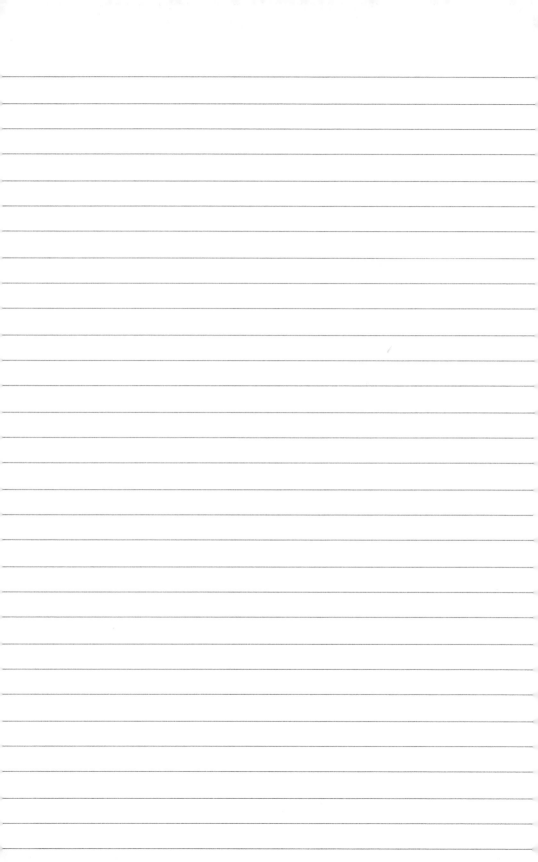

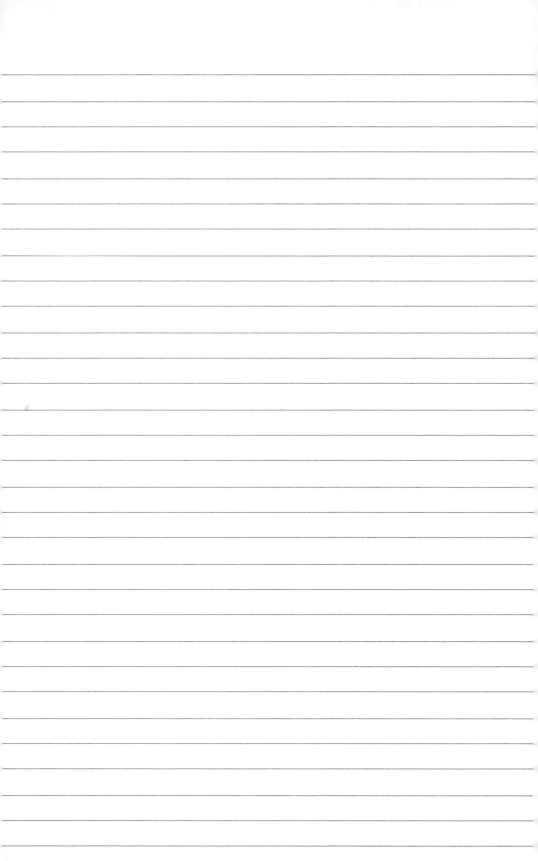

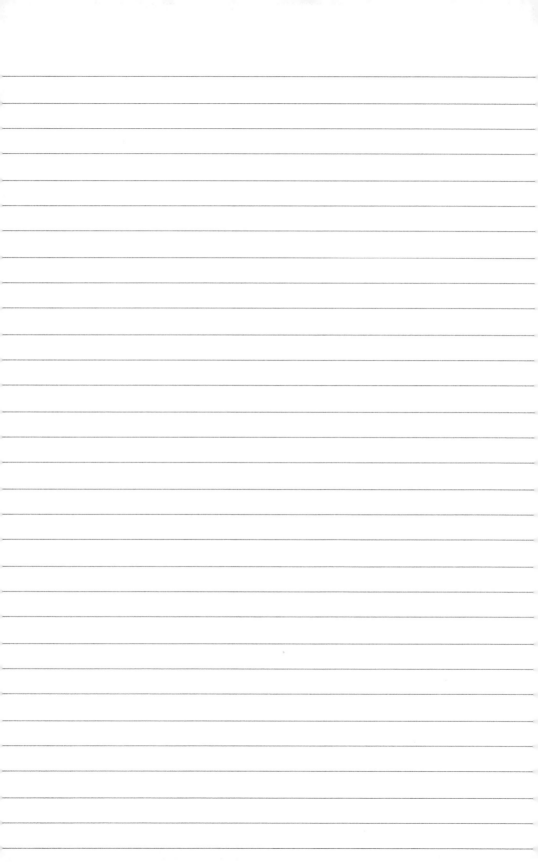

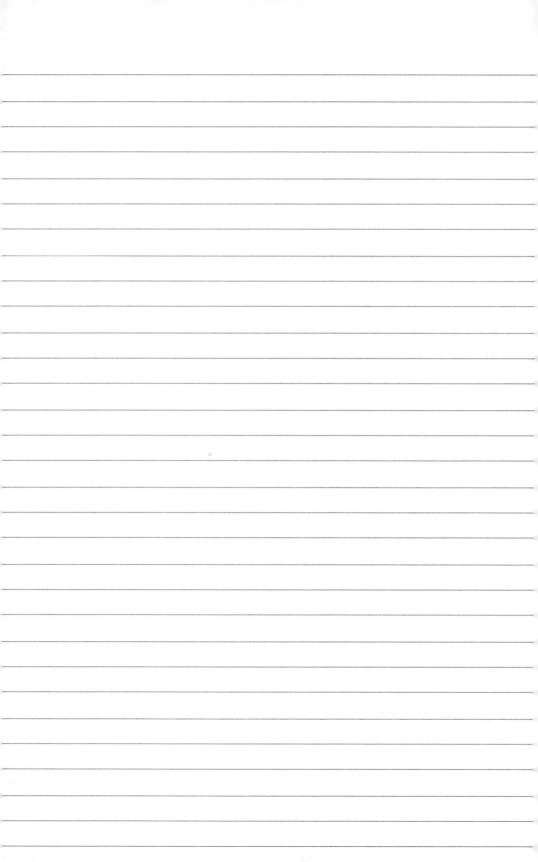

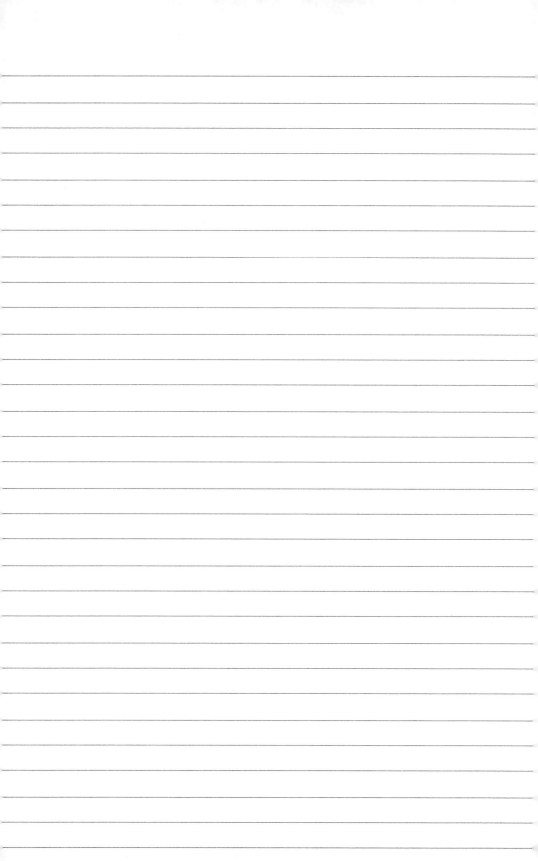

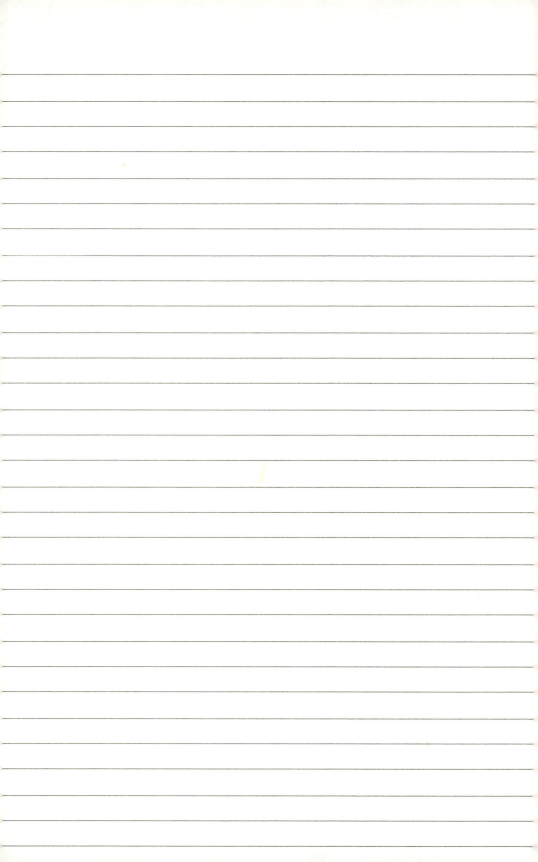

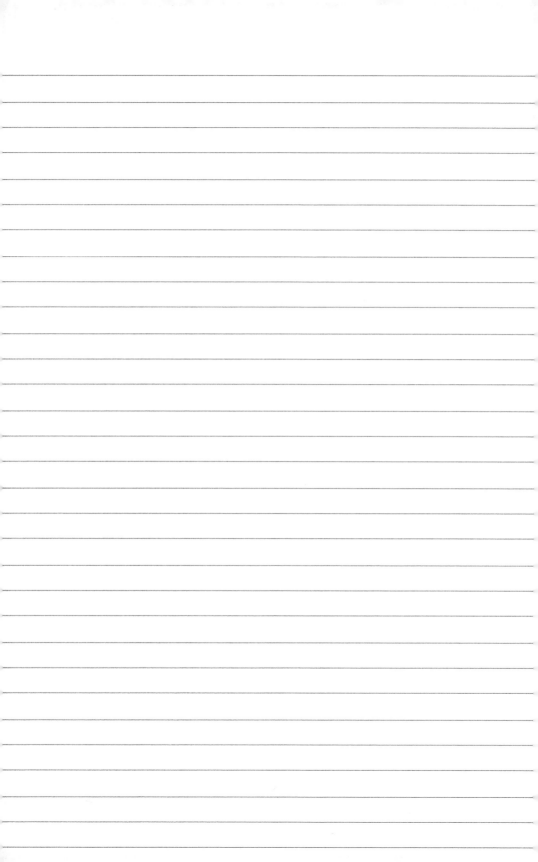

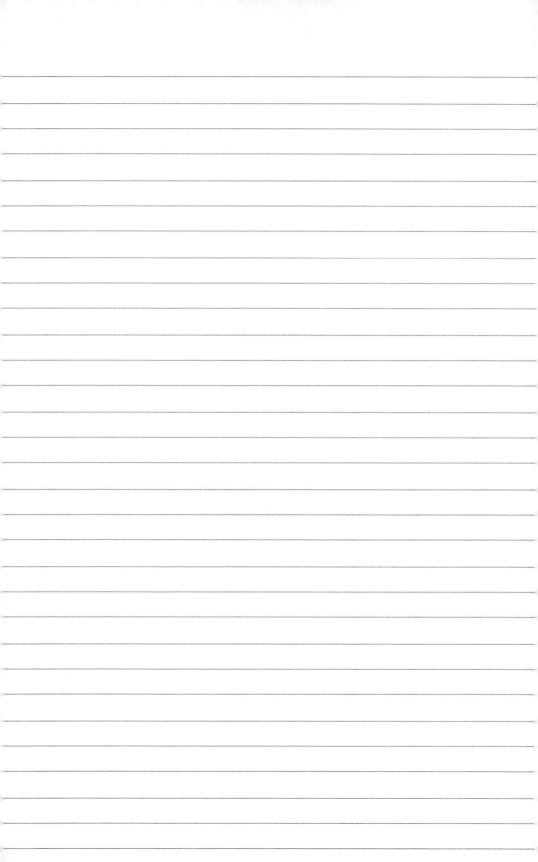

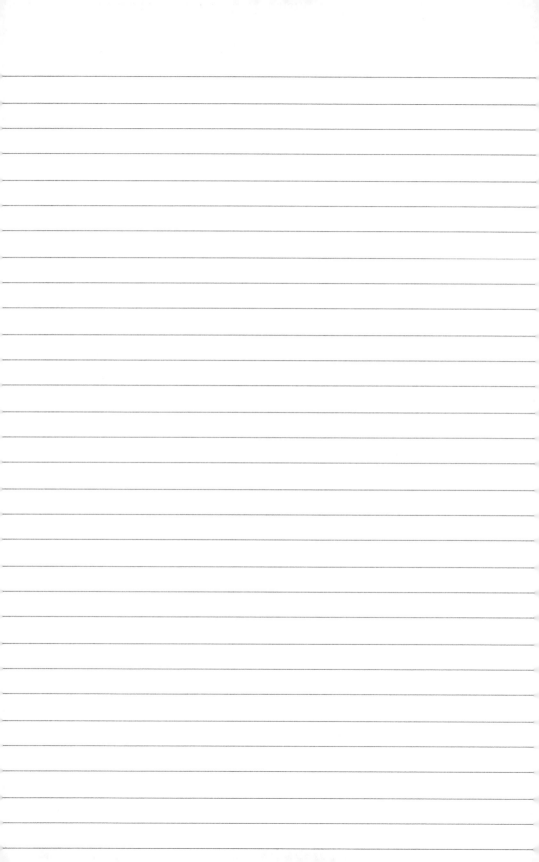

www.ingramcontent.com/pod-product-compliance
Lightning Source LLC
Chambersburg PA
CBHW051244050326
40689CB00007B/1058